Call Girls

A comedy

David Muncaster

New Theatre Publications - London

www.plays4theatre.com

2

3

© 2013 BY David Muncaster

First published in 2007

The edition published in 2013

New Theatre Publications

2 Hereford Close | Warrington | Cheshire | WA1 4HR | 01925 485605

www.plays4theatre.com   email: info@plays4theatre.com

New Theatre Publications is the trading name of the publishing house that is owned by members of the Playwrights' Co-operative. This innovative project was launched on the 1st October 1997 by writers Paul Beard and Ian Hornby with the aim of encouraging the writing and promotion of the very best in New Theatre by Professional and Amateur writers for the Professional and Amateur Theatre at home and abroad.

ISBN 9 781 840 94928 5

4

Characters

Mary
Jo
Tracy
Laura
Gary

7

Copyright Information

The play is fully protected under the Copyright laws of the British Commonwealth of Nations, the United States of America and all countries of the Berne and Universal Copyright Conventions.The play is fully protected under the Copyright laws of the British Commonwealth of Nations, the United States of America and all countries of the Berne and Universal Copyright Conventions.

All rights including Stage, Motion Picture, Radio, television, Public Reading, and Translation into Foreign Languages, are strictly reserved.

No part of this publication may lawfully be reproduced in ANY form or by any means - photocopying, typescript, recording (including video-recording), manuscript, electronic, mechanical or otherwise - or be transmitted or stored in a retrieval system, without prior permission.

Licenses for amateur performances are issued subject to the understanding that it shall be made clear in all advertising matter that the audience will witness an amateur performance; that the names of the authors of the plays shall be included on all programmes, and that the integrity of the authors' work will be preserved.

The Royalty Fee is subject to contract and subject to variation at the sole discretion of New Theatre Publications.

In Theatres of Halls seating Four Hundred or more the fee will be subject to negotiation.

In Territories Overseas the fee quoted may not apply. A fee will be quoted on application to New Theatre Publications, London.

Video-Recording of Amateur Productions

Please note that the copyright laws governing video-recording are extremely complex and that it should not be assumed that any play may be video-recorded for whatever purpose without first obtaining the permission of the appropriate agents. The fact that a play is published by New Theatre Publications does not indicate that video rights are available or that New Theatre Publications control such rights.

8

Performing Licence Applications

A performing licence for these plays will be issued by "New Theatre Publications" subject to the following conditions.

Conditions

1. That the performance fee is paid in full on the date of application for a licence.
2. That the name of the author(s) is/are clearly shown in any programme or publicity material.
3. That the author(s) is/are entitled to receive two complimentary tickets to see his/her/their work in performance if they so wish.
4. That a copy of the play is purchased from New Theatre Publications for each named speaking part and a minimum of three copies purchased for backstage use.
5. That a copy of any review be forwarded to New Theatre Publications.
6. That the New Theatre Publications logo is clearly shown on any publicity material. This is available on our website.

Fees

Details of script prices and fees payable for each performance or public reading can be obtained by telephone to (+44) 01925 485605 or to the address below.

Alternatively, latest prices can be obtained from our website www.plays4theatre.com where credit/debit cards can be used for payment.

To apply for a performing licence for any play please write to New Theatre Publications 2 Hereford Close, Warrington, Cheshire WA1 4HR or email info@plays4theatre.com with the following details:-

1. Name and address of theatre company.
2. Details of venue including seating capacity.
3. Dates of proposed performance or public reading.
4. Contact telephone number for Author's complimentary tickets.

Or apply directly via our website at www.plays4theatre.com

Call Girls
a comedy by David Muncaster
Synopsis

Call Girls is set in a call centre providing IT assistance to an unspecified company. Three of the women get on well together and 'have a laugh' but for the last six months their happy little group has been spoiled by the presence of Laura, an arrogant and aloof troublemaker whose predilection for short skirts and low cut tops probably has more to do with her getting the job than any particular work skills. Thankfully this is Laura's last week and the others decide not to let her go without letting her know exactly what they think of her. Surprisingly it is Mary, normally the quietist member of the group, who really lets rip but this uncharacteristic outburst could be the biggest mistake of her life.

Characters

Mary *is a quiet and nervous woman in her thirties or forties. She is the sort of woman who would remain silent in the company of strangers but is happy enough to contribute to the conversation when amongst friends.*

Jo *is a straightforward, sensible woman in her twenties or thirties and is Mary's best friend.*

Tracy *is similar to Jo but a bit more 'no nonsense'. She is confident and self assured and regards Jo and Mary as friends. She is in her twenties or thirties.*

Laura *is 'in your face' and arrogant. She dresses very seductively but without style. She is aloof from the rest of the group and really doesn't seem to care what anyone thinks of her. She is in her twenties or thirties.*

Gary *is disinterested in the day to day events in the office. He is aged between mid twenties and mid forties.*

The four women are seated at desks with computers in front of them. They are wearing telephone headsets. When a call comes though there is no audible ring and the mechanics of accepting and ending the call are controlled through the computer. This needs to be put over to the audience through exaggerated gestures. The action is continuous and takes place on a midweek morning.

Mary *(accepts a call)* Hello, helpdesk. *(Pause.)* Yes. Yes. Yes. Yes. *(Long pause.)* Yes. Yes. *(Pause. Quickly)* Yes. Yes. Yes. Yes. Yes. *(Pause.)* Yes. Goodbye. Thanks for calling.

Jo 'that Sally?

Mary Yes.

Jo Did she forget her password again?

Mary Yes.

Jo Then she remembered it?

Mary Yes.

Jo Silly cow.

Tracy *(accepts a call)* Hello, Helpdesk. *(Pause.)* And what were you doing when it happened? What do you mean you can't tell me? No, what were you doing on your computer? Have you rebooted? Switched it off and back on. Because it's called 'rebooting'. I didn't think I was spouting jargon at you. Well, OK. Try that and if it doesn't work call back. Thank you.

Jo Do you think Sally is lonely?

Tracy Sally who?

Jo The Sally who rings up everyday to say she's forgotten her password, then says, 'Oh, I just remembered it is broccoli'.

Mary Cabbage.

Jo What?

Mary She said her password was 'cabbage'.

Jo I'm saying nothing.

Tracy It's hardly the answer to loneliness is it? Ringing up a helpdesk and saying you've forgotten your password.

(Up to this point Laura has been ignoring the others, engrossed in her magazine until she is now alerted to a phone call.)

Laura *(accepts a call)* Yeah. Yeah the server was down. Try again in 10 mins.

(Jo and Mary exchange exasperated glances.)

Tracy Anyway, She probably likes being lonely. Veggies are like that.

Jo What?

Tracy You know. Veggies. Hang around in libraries, watch black and white movies. Burn candles whilst having a bath. Being lonely is part of the lifestyle.

Jo Not that you're generalising at all Tracy.

Mary How do you know she is a veggie?

Tracy Stands to reason. Her passwords are always vegetables.

Mary A tomato isn't a vegetable.

Tracy What?

Mary Her password was 'tomato' last week. A tomato is a fruit.

Tracy Thank you Alan Titchmarsh.

(The three of them laugh.)

Jo Perhaps being a veggie makes you forgetful.

Laura *(annoyed that the others have left her to pick up a call)* For God's sake. *(Accepts a call)* Y'ello. Yeah the server was down. Try again in 10.

Mary Do veggies eat fish?

Tracy Why?

Mary Cos it's brain food, isn't it?

Tracy And?

Mary So if she ate fish she wouldn't be so forgetful.

Tracy Good point Mary. I shall mention it to her next time she calls.

Laura Going for my break. *(Laura exits.)*

Jo How long has *she* got left.

Tracy She goes on Friday.

Jo Do you think she intends to tell everyone that the server has been down until then?

Tracy Wouldn't surprise me. It's about all she's done for the last six months.

Mary Phil is a veggie and he is a plasterer.

Tracy Oh Christ, Mary is off to planet Zog.

Jo What does being a plasterer have to do with anything?

Mary Well he doesn't hang around in libraries and burn candles when he's in the bath.

Jo How do you know?

Mary He's not the type.

Jo Come on Mary, let's hear it: when did you last share a bath with Phil?

Tracy Would somebody care to tell me: who the bloody hell is Phil?

Jo Mary's brother-in-law.

Tracy I see. So my argument crumbles. Well done Mary. I am a broken woman.

Jo   Did he ask you to soap his back?

Mary   Oh go and... *(Accepts a call)* Hello, helpdesk. Er yes... *(Looks at the others.)* We did have a problem on the server but it's fine now. Ok, can I take your name then. *(The conversation continues inaudibly.)*

Tracy   It'll be a relief when that Laura has gone, the lazy cow. She just makes more work for the rest of us.

Jo   It amazes me she's lasted so long.

Tracy   She knows her stuff you know. Bet she thinks this job is beneath her.

Jo   But Gary must of noticed that she doesn't do any work.

Tracy   All Gary's noticed is her tits.

Jo   Probably.

Mary   *(on the call)* Ok, thanks. An engineer will call you back. *(To the others)* They deserve it, some of them. His CD drive is not working and he believed her when she said it was a server problem.

Tracy   She's taking the proverbial though. I'm going to tell her when she comes back.

Mary   Oh no. Don't cause a fuss, it's only a few more days.

Tracy   All the more reason. Don't care if I upset her now cos I won't have to put up with her after this week.

Jo   Yay! Go Tracy!

Mary   Tracy.

Tracy   Oh, come on, Mary. Don't be a mouse all your life.

Mary   I am not a mouse.

Tracy   Really?

Mary   I'm not.

Tracy   So, how come you dream about Rick all day but you're too scared to 'squeak' to him?

Mary   That's got nothing to do with what we are talking about.

Tracy   Yes it does. We are talking about you being a mouse.

Jo   You have to admit Mary, it's about time something happened there. How long have you been on about him? Why don't you just ask him out?

Mary It's not up to me to make the first move. The man should do that.

Jo How quaint. Oh, you are old fashioned.

Mary What's wrong with being old fashioned?

Tracy Oh my God! I've just had this vision of Rick walking in here in his caveman suit and bumping you over the head with his club before dragging you off by your hair.

Jo *(to Tracy)* So long as it's his club. *(They laugh.)*

Mary When you have finished laughing at my expense!

Tracy Oh, lighten up Mary.

Mary Well. Rick's got nothing to do with what we are talking about and anyway, I don't dream about him all day. I merely mentioned, once, that I liked him and that was because you insisted on questioning me about my likes and dislikes, so can we just leave it?

Tracy Ooooh!

Mary I mean it.

Jo Girls. Girls. Let's not fall out. We were talking about Laura.

Mary Yes. Yes we were. She is the cause of all this. But I just want to make the point: I am not a mouse!

Tracy Ok Mary, agreed. So, are you going to hold her whilst I thump her then?

Mary She won't be here next week Tracy. Just bide your time.

Tracy And let her go thinking she's better than us? No, I'm going to wipe that smug grin off her face.

Jo So, what are you going to say?

Tracy I just want to remind her that she is supposed to be part of a team here.

Mary Ok then. But don't get into trouble.

Tracy You know me. My middle name is tact. Anyway, it's ok. If I get done, I'll say you put me up to it.

(Mary shudders but she knows Tracy is joking.)

Jo She's coming.

(Laura enters.)

Tracy Had a good break?

Laura What?

Tracy I said, have you had a good break?

Laura It was ok. If you can call sitting in crap caff with a bunch of morons ok.

Tracy So, you'll be refreshed and ready to go now then?

Laura What the hell are you on about?

Tracy I mean, you are ready to do your share.

Laura I take more calls then you do Tracy Jones. More than the rest of you put together. You lot should hear yourselves sometimes. You're so busy talking crap you don't even notice the calls coming in.

Tracy I do my share. We all do. And at least I try to help the customers. I don't just give them the brush off.

Laura What's that supposed to mean?

Tracy (mimicking) 'The server's been down'. Do you think we don't hear you?

Laura Well for your information the server was down this morning. You didn't know that did you? If you read the reports instead of treating this place like some sort of kindergarten you might be able to do a half decent job.

Tracy How dare you? I've never seen you paying any attention to reports. I bet Gary told you the server had been down when you took him a cuppa this morning. I notice you never think to ask us if we would like a cup of tea bringing.

Laura And just what the hell has it got to do with you anyway? Just who do you think you are? You've been here since the year dot. And where's it got you? Nowhere. Don't you tell me how to do my job. I could eat you and spit you out.

Jo (Accepts a call) Hello, helpdesk.

Tracy Oh, come on. You're only here because you flaunt your body to Gary. If you dressed decently you would have been out months ago.

Laura (with mock shock) Hah. You ugly bitch!

Tracy Oh, grow up. Why not change the habit of a lifetime and do a bit of work for your last few days?

Laura So says Miss Productivity.

Tracy I do my share.

Laura Yeah, right. None of you are ever likely to break into a sweat are you? Even when you can be bothered to put in a full day. (Laura *gives Mary a scornful look.)*

Mary   *(pretending to accept a call)* Er, hello, helpdesk. *(Nervously, in a squeaky voice)* Yes, can I help you?

Tracy   Bitch!

Laura   Cow!

Tracy   Tart!

Mary   *(still pretending to be on a call)* Um. I'm, er, sorry to hear that. Er...

Jo   *(on the call)* No problem. Goodbye. *(To Laura)* Look. Keep your voice down, they can hear you down the phone.

Laura   It's ok. I think Big Mouth has run out of steam. *(She sits down and picks up her magazine.)*

Mary   *(still pretending to be on a call)* And when did it start to do that?

Jo   Mary.

Mary   Uh? *(Jo pulls a face)* I'm on a call. *(down the phone)* Yes, I'm still here.

Gary   *(enters.)* Incredible Mary. According to the system, we don't have any incoming calls, but here you are jabbering away. Do you have a telepathic link?

(Mary looks sheepish and is about to try to think up some excuse but Gary turns his back to her and faces Laura.)

Gary   Laura. Could you come to my office for a moment?

(Gary and Laura exit. The remaining three look at each other and eventually Jo speaks.)

Jo   What do you think?

Tracy   Well he must have heard us.

Jo   So, why didn't he take both of you?

Tracy   Well, perhaps we've underestimated the man. Maybe he *can* see past her tits after all.

Jo   I hope so. I bet she's in there calling you every name under the sun.

Tracy   Let her. What can he do to me anyway?

Jo   She'll say you started it

Tracy   And I'll say she's a lazy old tart.

(Jo and Tracy look at each other for a moment then burst out laughing.)

Mary   I don't know why you're laughing. You could be in trouble.

Tracy   Your call finished has it, Mary?

(Jo and Tracy laugh.)

Mary   I… Well I…

Tracy   Yes?

Mary   Oh shut up.

(All three laugh.)

Jo   Your face when she called you an ugly bitch. I really thought you were going to hit her.

Tracy   What do you mean? *(Smiling)* I was totally in control.

Mary   So. Do you think she is, you know, getting the boot?

Tracy   I expect so. Should have been months ago but at least we will be spared her last few days.

Jo   Where is she going anyway? Did she say?

Tracy   I never bothered to ask her. To be honest I don't think Gary would have said anything if I hadn't seen her job advertised. When he said: 'Laura will be moving on', I was just grateful.

Mary   Do you think they'll still take her? You know, if she gets sacked from here.

Tracy   Don't know, don't care.

Mary   I hope she is alright.

Jo   Oh Mary!

Mary   Well, I know she is lazy and she's never tried to fit in but, like you say, she knows her stuff so she must have been frustrated in a lowly job like this. I didn't like her but I don't wish her any harm.

Tracy   That's very noble of you.

Mary   Well. She's never done me any harm.

Tracy   Oh. Really.

Jo   Tracy.

Mary   What?

Jo   Nothing.

Mary   What?

Jo   Forget it.

Mary   Tell me.

Tracy   She told Gary about you leaving early.

Mary   I don't leave early.

Tracy   I know. But the rules say you have to take breaks at the allotted time. You can't take your break 15 minutes before the end of your shift and go home.

Mary   But the bus...

Tracy   Yes dear. I know, I know and we don't mind but Gary came in here late one afternoon the other day and asked where you were. Jo said you had to go and it was a one off but you could tell he didn't believe it and then he looked at Laura and she smiled that smug smile of hers and we realised she had dropped you in it.

Mary   So, why didn't you tell me?

Tracy   We thought, if he didn't say anything to you the next day then it meant he would turn a blind eye. And I think he has.

Mary   Has he?

Tracy   Well he hasn't said anything to you has he?

Mary   Oh God.

Jo   Don't worry Mary, dear. He knows you are a good worker. I bet he has thought it over and decided not to worry about it. Turn a blind eye, like Tracy says.

Mary   I know what he thinks. He thinks I'm a mouse. That's what he thinks. Just like you said. I'm a mouse. He thinks he'll store that one up and use it against me when he feels like it. Well, I'm not a mouse. I'm going to tell him that I have to finish ten minutes early and if he doesn't like it he can stick his job!

Jo   Mary!

Mary   You think I don't have it in me, don't you?

Jo   It's not that, it's..

Mary   I'm not a mouse, Jo. I'm not being trampled on anymore. *(Accepts a call.)* Yes. Yes the server was down. Try again in ten minutes.

Jo & Tracy *(together)* Mary!

Mary   I am not a mouse!

(The three sit in silence for a while then Tracy tries to break the ice.)

Tracy   It is quiet this morning.

Jo   Oh don't use the Q word. You'll tempt fate.

Tracy   Still, it can get boring though. Mind you, we have a laugh don't we?

Jo   Yeah, we have a laugh.

Tracy   Don't you agree, Mary? We have a laugh. *(Mary does not answer.)* Wonder what the new girl will be like. Laura's replacement.

Jo   Might be a bloke.

Tracy   Now you're talking. A handsome young grad. Trying to break into IT.

Jo   Bit shy. Not nerdy but not bit nervous of being surrounded by women.

Tracy   But he secretly has a crush one of them.

Jo   Or two of them.

Tracy   Or three of them. *(They look at Mary who is staring out front, ignoring them.)* Then comes the Christmas party.

Jo   He gets a bit tipsy. Makes a pass.

Tracy   Ends up doing something he shouldn't.

Jo   And feels terrible about it after.

Tracy   Not realising that he has been manoeuvred into it by a couple of old tarts.

(Jo and Tracy laugh.)

Tracy   Bet it'll be some old hag. Handsome young grads don't go into IT these days. It isn't sexy to work in IT anymore.

Jo   You're right. It's all geeks and saddos these days.

Tracy   Ahem.

Jo   Present company excepted.

Tracy   Thank you.

(Gary and Laura enter. Laura goes to her desk and starts to collect her things. After a while Mary stands up and crosses to her.)

Mary   So. You finally got your comeuppance did you? Well good riddance. It takes a lot to get me riled but I don't like sneaks and I don't like two faced cows. We were happy here. A good team, we all got along fine, then you come along with your short skirts and your tits in everyone's face and you try to rock the boat.

Well, it hasn't worked out for you, has it? You've been found out. You're lazy, you're rude and you're rubbish at your job. I just hope that your new employers see through you a bit quicker, that's all. *(With a final burst, almost shrieking)* Now get out of my sight, you cow!

(Laura smiles slightly and sits down at the desk. Gary steps forward.)

Gary   I was going to announce this on Friday afternoon but due to this morning's events, I thought it wise to bring it forward. I am leaving the company. Laura takes over from me from Monday.

(Jo and Tracy look at each other disbelievingly whilst Mary staggers slowly back to her chair as the curtain falls.)

More Plays by David Muncaster

Community Spirit

Full Length Farce - 8m 3f

The village of Snickerton has a new community hall and all the local groups get together to organise an opening day that will never be forgotten. Pity Mel, the poor official from the local council who has to try to keep apart the warring factions.

There is Mike, the bombastic chairman from the choral society, who clashes with Chris, his deadly rival, as well as just about anyone else who dare to disagree with him. Add a couple of luvies from the am dram, some representatives of Churches Together who couldn't be further apart, the leader of the cubs and beavers who sees things in the night, and a host of other characters including a caretaker with a very unfortunate name.

Community Spirit is a large cast play with eleven speaking roles and any number of none speaking roles that starts out as a comedy of manners but by the end is pure farce.

Great fun for any theatre group looking to involve as many of their members as possible.

Mad Gary's Fruit and Nut Case

Full Length Comedy Thriller - 4m 4f

It is a big day for Tommy. His lovely daughter Peaches has just married Lionel Looselips, the son of the biggest fruit and veg wholesale magnate in the whole of the county. Now Tommy can be assured that his market stall will always have the freshest, best value produce known to man. The wedding reception is a grand affair, friends and relations are joined by rivals who, for one day, put their differences aside; or do they? As the ceremonial fruit salad is consumed the guests start dropping like fruit flies.

Who is responsible for this murderous act? What did they hope to gain? Who will be next? It's a job for "Mad" Gary Grasslover of the local constabulary. This intentionally corny and ribald comedy/murder mystery provides plenty of laughs and opportunity for the audience to join in the fun by, not only trying to guess the murderer, but also by selected members being given characters to play.

Waiting for a Train

Full Length Play - 4f

Set on the platform of a rural railway station waiting for a train that never comes, this is a play about life, love and hope. The stark reality of living with schizophrenia is contrasted by the warmth and playfulness that exists between the main characters. With a degree of flexibility in casting and a set that would work better if it is suggested rather than detailed this is play should be relatively simple to stage at the same time giving the actors the opportunity to immerse themselves into characters that have great complexity and depth.

Fresh Showers for the Thirsting Flowers

One Act Play - 2f

Alice is a retired English teacher who is living a comfortable if rather lonely existence. A chance encounter with her neighbour's daughter re-awakens her passion to teach when she discovers that most unusual of things. A pupil who wants to learn! With a respectful nod to 'Educating Rita' this is a story of how a generation gap is easily bridged through the discovery of a mutual interest. All scenes are set in Alice`s living room which has minimal set requirements. The title of this play is taken from the poem 'The Cloud' by Percy Bysshe Shelley. Other quotes in this play are considered 'fair usage' and do not contravene copyright law but a licence is required to use the music specified.

Mission Impossible (Long Version)

One Act Play - 2m 3f

A meeting room, a flip chart, an enthusiastic facilitator, and four employees who are determined to give her a hard time. This is the background to Mission Impossible, a hilarious look at the corporate nonsense that anyone who has ever attended a team bonding session will know only too well. Ice Breakers and silly games do little to bond this team as the beleaguered facilitator gets tough to ensure that she gets the outcome she desires. Mission Impossible won the Congleton One Act Play Festival 2009. This is an extended version of the original play and is a little bit longer, a little bit ruder and quite a bit sillier.

The only monthly magazine passionate about amateur theatre

www.ingramcontent.com/pod-product-compliance
Lightning Source LLC
Chambersburg PA
CBHW060608030426

42337CB00019B/3659